SPEAK & SPELL

SIDE B

Photographic
Tora! Tora! Tora!
Big Muff
Any Second Now (Voices)
Just Can't Get Enough

DEPECHE M●DE

The Unauthorized Biography

Written by Soledad Romero Mariño
Illustrated by Fernando López del Hierro

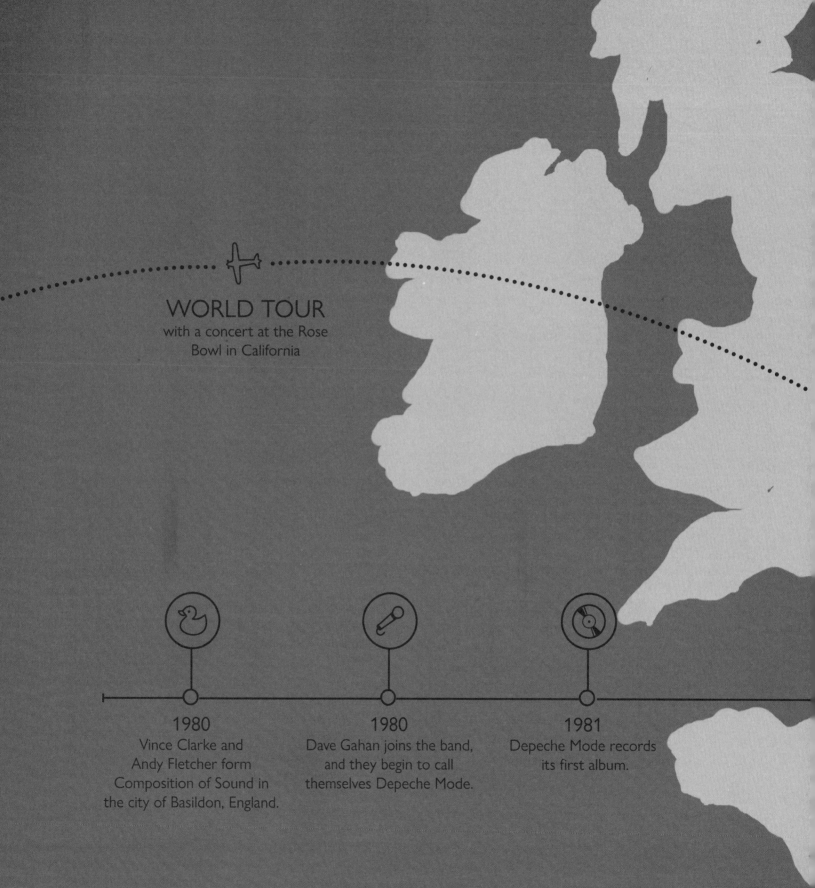

WORLD TOUR
with a concert at the Rose
Bowl in California

1980
Vince Clarke and
Andy Fletcher form
Composition of Sound in
the city of Basildon, England.

1980
Dave Gahan joins the band,
and they begin to call
themselves Depeche Mode.

1981
Depeche Mode records
its first album.

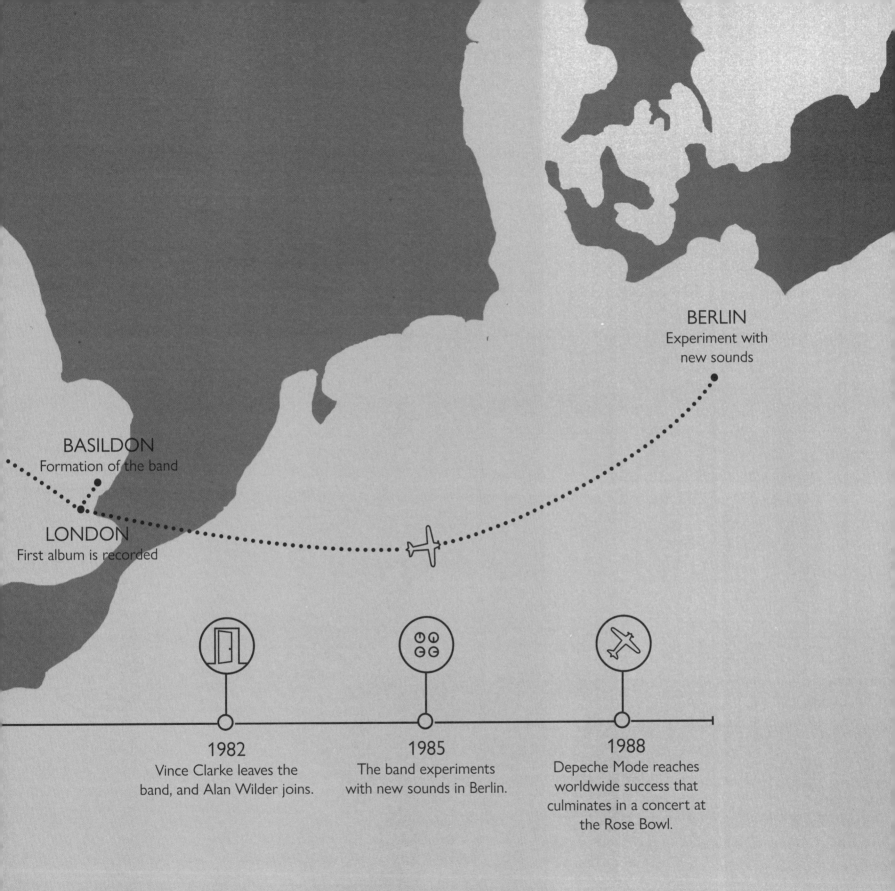

BERLIN
Experiment with new sounds

BASILDON
Formation of the band

LONDON
First album is recorded

1982
Vince Clarke leaves the band, and Alan Wilder joins.

1985
The band experiments with new sounds in Berlin.

1988
Depeche Mode reaches worldwide success that culminates in a concert at the Rose Bowl.

CHURCH

Basildon, a large and bustling town, lay just beyond the railroad tracks thirty miles east of London.

Every evening in the church, the voices of the choir could be heard practicing the songs they would perform on Sunday.

Among the young singers, friends Vince Clarke and Andy Fletcher were about to change their lives completely.

CHELMSFORD FESTIVAL

It began during the spring of 1979, when Vince had not yet turned twenty and had big dreams for the world.

The English teenager, who was a little rebellious, took the train to his first punk festival in England. The Chelmsford Festival was a massive party with loud music playing and young people enjoying their freedom. Vince had never seen anything like it!

On the ride back home, Vince sat in the back of the train car, and a new idea started running through his head.

When he arrived at the Basildon station with confidence in his step, Vince's new dream had begun. He left the church choir, changed the style of his hair and his clothes, and started his own band.

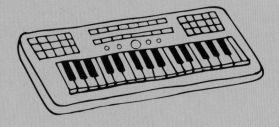

SYNTHESIZER BAND

After some early attempts, Vince and his friend Andy created Composition of Sound.

In their music, they used synthesizers, new electronic instruments that could create an endless number of sounds and that were much easier to play than traditional instruments.

Their next step was signing Martin Gore, a classmate from Andy's school. Martin was passionate about music and, most importantly at that time, was about to buy a synthesizer.

Vince and Andy went with Martin to buy it. They walked and talked excitedly on the way to the store. Behind the glass case rested the wonderful, gleaming instrument.

They came home overjoyed—they had in their hands the new Yamaha CS-5.

FIRST REHEARSALS

Martin broke open the cardboard box and uncovered his new instrument. He connected the wires, plugged it in, and turned it on. With so many keys and buttons, it was hard to know where to start. He softly pressed a key at random, and a breathtaking sound filled the room.

Martin, Vince, and Andy immediately began to rehearse at home with an improvised stage. With the instruments plugged in and the young men in their positions, an expectant audience of friends, girlfriends, brothers, and pets listened, fascinated by the modern sound of the teenage band.

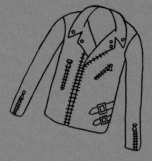

DAVE GAHAN

Soon they rented a rehearsal room that they shared with other bands.

One day between rehearsals, a dark-haired boy with a leather jacket took the microphone. Without music and in a low voice, he sang "Heroes" by David Bowie, one of the most beautiful love songs ever written.

Vince heard him from the doorway. Vince was stunned, and as he watched, enraptured, he knew that was the voice he was looking for. The dark-haired boy's name was Dave Gahan, and by the following week, he was part of the band.

DEPECHE MODE

In Concert

The Bridgehouse
Thursday,
October 16th

DEPECHE MODE

The band was finally complete with Vince, Andy, Martin, and Dave. They were young, modern, and talented. They went out on stage in the latest fashion, wearing leather pants, silk shirts, silver ties, and black boots. They were progressive, and so was their music and their fashion. They decided to call themselves Depeche Mode, which in French means "fashion news."

Within a few weeks, Depeche Mode would be performing in London. The electronic rhythms pulsed in people's bodies, and the catchy songs drove the teenagers crazy.

FIRST ALBUM

Electronic music came like a wave, and the group was a sensation on the stage. In less than a year, Depeche Mode managed to record their first album.

Vince composed upbeat melodies, Andy and Martin followed with futuristic rhythms, and Dave brought emotion and color with his irresistible voice. The album was modern and danceable electronic pop music, an incredible thirty-nine minutes of bubbling songs.

VINCE CLARKE

And then one day, everything changed. "I never thought we would be so successful. I'm not happy," Vince Clarke confessed to his bandmates after a concert.

It was devastating, and nobody could believe it—the leader of the band had abandoned them. Magazines wrote about the news, radio shows discussed it, and fans cried sadly for the loss. Everyone thought the teenage dream was at an end.

But they were wrong.

Martin Gore took the reins of composing. The songs stopped being colorful and happy, and a new, dark, and deep style would emerge for Depeche Mode.

ALAN WILDER

To replace Vince at concerts, Depeche Mode looked for an expert with the machines. Without a doubt, Alan Wilder was a phenomenon, sometimes even playing three or four keyboards at a time.

He was tall, attractive, and had an undeniable talent that caused fainting in his path. He could build universes of sound effects, instruments, voices, and echoes. At first he only played in the live shows, but thanks to his creativity, he

ELECTRONIC POP MUSIC

The nightclub was more than full—people wearing bright shirts, bangs, hairspray, and shoulder pads packed the floor. The DJ took out the record, uncovered it, and put it on the turntable. The radiant vinyl began to turn, and the young people could not stop dancing.

Depeche Mode was wildy popular in the dance clubs, but the band members made an effort to be much more than a pop band to dance to. They took the message of their lyrics and the injustices of the world very seriously.

BERLIN

In 1985, Depeche Mode recorded an album in Berlin. At the time, a wall divided the city in two. The east side was orderly, silent, and boring. The west side was chaotic, boisterous, and fun. The recording studio was on the west side, in a crumbling, faded building.

Berlin was the perfect scene for innovation. The young men recorded all kinds of noises there, like the melody of a doll, the whistle of a coffee machine, and the rattle of an old motorcycle... a feast of sounds that, when mixed in their machines, became rhythms and melodies that seemed to come from other galaxies.

101

Martin, Dave, Andy, and Alan toured the world's stages, recorded albums, had the applause of critics, and appeared in magazines.

In June 1988, Depeche Mode conquered America. The band entered the great Rose Bowl stadium in a fire-red convertible with leather upholstery. They played the 101st concert of their great world tour, an epic spectacle that none of the sixty-five thousand people who saw it will ever forget.

Depeche Mode were and always will be the secret influence behind decades of metal music, critics of the greed of humanity, and the warriors of modern electronic music.

DEPECHE MODE STUDIO ALBUMS

- ⊙ SPEAK & SPELL (1981)

- ⊙ A BROKEN FRAME (1982)

- ⊙ CONSTRUCTION TIME AGAIN (1983)

- ⊙ SOME GREAT REWARD (1984)

- ⊙ BLACK CELEBRATION (1986)

- ⊙ MUSIC FOR THE MASSES (1987)

◎ VIOLATOR (1990)

◎ SONGS OF FAITH AND
DEVOTION (1993)

◎ ULTRA (1997)

◎ EXCITER (2001)

◎ PLAYING THE ANGEL (2005)

◎ SOUNDS OF THE UNIVERSE (2009)

◎ DELTA MACHINE (2013)

◎ SPIRIT (2017)

LEARN MORE ABOUT
THE HISTORY OF MUSIC
WITH THESE GREAT BOOKS.

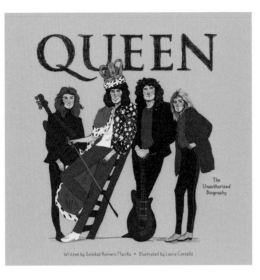

The origin of one of the most ambitious and theatrical rock bands.

The incredible story of four friends who became legends of punk rock.

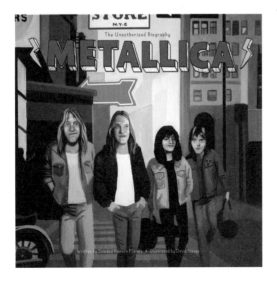

The electrifying adventure of the band that challenged metal's limits.

Scan here to listen to Depeche Mode's first LP

First published in the United States in 2020 by Sourcebooks

Published by Sourcebooks eXplore, an imprint of Sourcebooks Kids
P.O. Box 4410, Naperville, Illinois 60567–4410
(630) 961-3900
sourcebookskids.com

Originally published as Band Records: *Depeche Mode* in 2018 by Reservoir Kids, an imprint of Penguin Random House Grupo Editorial.

Library of Congress Cataloging-in-Publication Data is on file with the publisher.

Source of Production: PrintPlus Limited, Shenzhen, Guangdong Province, China
Date of Production: April 2020
Run Number: 5018392

Printed and bound in China.
PP 10 9 8 7 6 5 4 3 2 1

SPEAK & SPELL

SIDE A

New Life
I Sometimes Wish I Was Dead
Puppets
Boys Say Go!
Nodisco
What's Your Name?